D1365829

DRAGONS

DRAGONS

An Anthology of Verse
❦ and Prose ❦

SMITHMARK

© Anness Publishing Limited 1996

All rights reserved. No part of this publication may be
reproduced, stored in a retrieval system, or transmitted in
any way or by any means, electronic, mechanical,
photocopying, recording or otherwise, without the prior
permission of the copyright owner.

This edition published in 1996 by
Smithmark Publishers, a division of U.S. Media Holdings, Inc.,
16 East 32nd Street,
New York,
NY 10016.

SMITHMARK books are available for bulk purchase for sales
promotion and for premium use. For details write or call
the manager of special sales, SMITHMARK Publishers Inc.
16 East 32nd Street, New York, 10016; (212) 532-6600

Produced by Anness Publishing Limited
1 Boundary Row
London SE1 8HP

Printed in Singapore by Star Standard Industries Private Ltd.

10 9 8 7 6 5 4 3 2 1

CONTENTS

BIBLICAL DRAGONS

The dragon is not only one of the oldest of all mythical beasts; it has a place in nearly every mythology, often as a symbol of evil. In the Old Testament the dragon, or serpent, represented the Devil himself.

LEVIATHAN

I WILL NOT conceal his parts,
Nor his power, nor his comely proportion.
Who can discover the face of his garment?
Or who can come to him with his double bridle?
Who can open the doors of his face?
His teeth are terrible round about.
His scales are his pride,
Shut up together as with a close seal.
One is so near to another,
That no air can come between them.
They are joined one to another,
They stick together, that they cannot be sundered.
By his neesings a light doth shine,
And his eyes are like the eyelids of the morning.
Out of his mouth go burning lamps,
And sparks of fire leap out.
Out of his nostrils goeth smoke,
As out of a seething pot or caldron.
His breath kindleth coals,
And a flame goeth out of his mouth.
In his neck remaineth strength,
And sorrow is turned into joy before him.
The flakes of his flesh are joined together:
They are firm in themselves; they cannot be moved.
His heart is as firm as a stone;
Yea, as hard as a piece of the nether mill-stone.
When he raiseth up himself, the mighty are afraid.
By reason of breakings they purify themselves.
The sword of him that layeth at him cannot hold:
The spear, the dart, nor the habergeon.
He esteemeth iron as straw,
And brass as rotten wood.
The arrow cannot make him flee:
Slingstones are turned with him into stubble.
Darts are counted as stubble:
He laugheth at the shaking of a spear.
Sharp stones are under him:
He spreadeth sharp pointed things upon the mire.
He maketh the deep to boil like a pot:
He maketh the sea like a pot of ointment.
He maketh a path to shine after him;
One would think the deep to be hoary.
Upon earth there is not his like,
Who is made without fear.
He beholdeth all high things:
He is a king over all the children of pride.

THE BOOK OF JOB, XLI, 12–34

THE DRAGON CHAINED

And I saw an angel come down from heaven, having the key of the bottomless pit and a great chain in his hand. And he laid hold on the dragon, the old serpent, which is the Devil, and Satan, and bound him a thousand years, and cast him into the bottomless pit, and shut him up, and set a seal upon him, that he should deceive the nations no more, till the thousand years should be fulfilled: and after that he must be loosed a little season.

THE REVELATION, XX, 1-3

See the old dragon from his throne
Sink with enormous ruin down!

PHILIP.DODDRIDGE (1702-1751), *HYMN*

12

St Michael and the Dragon

And there appeared another wonder in heaven; and behold a great red dragon, having seven heads and ten horns, and seven crowns upon his heads. And his tail drew the third part of the stars of heaven, and did cast them to the earth: and the dragon stood before the woman which was ready to be delivered, for to devour her child as soon as it was born. And she brought forth a man child, who was to rule all nations with a rod of iron: and her child was caught up unto God, and to his throne. And the woman fled into the wilderness, where she hath a place prepared of God, that they should feed her there a thousand two hundred and threescore days.

And there was war in heaven: Michael and his angels fought against the dragon; and the dragon fought and his angels, and prevailed not; neither was their place found any more in heaven. And the great dragon was cast out, that old serpent, called the Devil, and Satan, which deceiveth the whole world: he was cast out into the earth, and his angels were cast out with him ...

THE REVELATION, XII, 1-9

ⱭND THE DRⱭGON WⱭS WROTH

And when the dragon saw that he was cast unto the earth, he persecuted the woman which brought forth the man child. And to the woman were given two wings of a great eagle, that she might fly into the wilderness, into her place, where she is nourished for a time, and times, and half a time, from the face of the serpent. And the serpent cast out of his mouth water as a flood after the woman, that he might cause her to be carried away of the flood. And the earth helped the woman, and the earth opened her mouth, and swallowed up the flood which the dragon cast out of his mouth. And the dragon was wroth with the woman, and went to make war with the remnant of her seed, which keep the commandments of God, and have the testimony of Jesus Christ.

THE REVELATION, XII, 13-17

Dragons of Ancient Greece

In Greek mythology the dragon was not so much a symbol as the ultimate heroic assignment. Sooner or later every warrior had to test his mettle against this terrifying adversary, the odds improved now and then by a little outside help.

Typhon, the Child of Earth

His hands are busy with the works of strength, and unwearied are the mighty God's feet: and from his shoulders grew a hundred serpent heads, heads of a dread dragon that licked with dusky tongues, and from the eyes of his wondrous heads fire flashed beneath his brows, and from all his heads fire burned as he glared. And in all his terrible heads were voices that uttered all manner of cries unspeakable. Sometimes they uttered such sounds as the gods might understand: anon the roar of a bellowing bull, proud and untamable of spirit: sometimes, again, the roaring of a lion of dauntless heart: sometimes noises as of whelps, wondrous to hear: and anon he would hiss, and the high hills echoed to the sound.

HESIOD, *THEOGONY*

Hercules and the Lernean Hydra

As a second labour Eurystheus ordered Hercules to kill the Lernean hydra. That creature, bred in the swamp of Lerna, used to go forth into the plain and ravage both the cattle and the country. Now the hydra had a huge body, with nine heads, eight mortal, but the middle one immortal. So mounting a chariot driven by Iolaus, he came to Lerna, and having halted his horses, he discovered the hydra on a hill beside the springs of the Amymone, where was its den. By pelting it with fiery shafts he forced it to come out, and in the act of doing so he seized and held it fast. But the hydra wound itself around one of his feet and clung to him. Nor could he effect anything by smashing its heads with his club, for as fast as one head was smashed there grew up two. A huge crab also came to the help of the hydra by biting his foot. So he killed it, and in his turn called for help on Iolaus who, by setting fire to a piece of the neighbouring wood and burning the roots of the heads with the brands, prevented them from sprouting. Having thus got the better of the sprouting heads, he chopped off the immortal head, and buried it, and put a heavy rock on it, beside the road that leads through Lerna to Elaeus.

Apollodorus, *The Library*

PERSEUS AND THE SEA MONSTER

Bidding farewell to the Hesperides, Perseus winged his way towards the east, and came at last to the seashore. And there he saw a maiden, chained to a rock well out at sea. Wonderingly, Perseus flew towards her, and, coming nearer, found her to be a beautiful princess, whose long, flowing hair was her only clothing. The waves and the rising tide swept round her, and her frightened face made Perseus hasten to her, more especially as, coming nearer and nearer, he saw the winding form of a great dragon approaching her.

Perseus swooped down, and the people thronging the shore heard the howls of the serpent, the clash of a sword upon its scales, saw the lashing tail churn the water into foam, and knew that some stranger hero had come to save the unfortunate princess. The fight between the dragon and Perseus lasted for a long time, and the shackled maiden looked on with straining eyes, seeking to discover who it was that fought so valiantly to save her from the beast which had come up to devour her.

At last the gallant Perseus won – the dragon, fighting to the end, lay dead in the reddened sea, turned to stone! For Perseus, realizing that he stood little chance of overcoming the monster by ordinary means, had suddenly opened the magic pouch, and held Medusa's head before the eyes of the dragon. The crowd on shore ran down to the rock. Here they saw the sandalled Perseus, who had taken off his magic cap, and they marvelled at this man who had overcome the dragon.

CHRISTINE CHAUNDLER,
MY BOOK OF BEAUTIFUL LEGENDS

THE GUARDIAN OF THE GOLDEN FLEECE

But you know not," said Medeia, "what he must do who would win the fleece. He must tame the two brazen-footed bulls, who breathe devouring flame; and with them he must plough ere nightfall four acres in the field of Ares; and he must sow them with serpents' teeth, of which each tooth springs up into an armed man. Then he must fight with all those warriors; and little will it profit him to conquer them, for the fleece is guarded by a serpent, more huge than any mountain pine; and over his body you must step if you would reach the golden fleece." ...

Medeia and the heroes ran forward and hurried through the poison wood, among the dark stems of the mighty beeches, guided by the gleam of the golden fleece, until they saw it hanging on one vast tree in the midst. And Jason would have sprung to seize it; but Medeia held him back, and pointed, shuddering, to the tree-foot, where the mighty serpent lay, coiled in and out among the roots, with a body like a mountain pine. His coils stretched many a fathom, spangled with bronze and gold; and half of him they could see, but no more, for the rest lay in darkness far beyond.

And when he saw them coming he lifted up his head, and watched them with his small bright eyes, and flashed his forked tongue, and roared like the fire among the woodlands, till the forest tossed and groaned. For his cries shook the trees from leaf to root, and swept over the long reaches of the river, and over Aietes' hall, and woke the sleepers in the city, till mothers clasped their children in their fear.

CHARLES KINGSLEY, *THE HEROES*

Jason and Medea

Hideous he was, where all things else were fair;
Dull-skinned, foul-spotted, with lank rusty hair
About his neck; and hooked yellow claws
Just showed from 'neath his belly and huge jaws,
Closed in the hideous semblance of a smile.
Then Jason shuddered, wondering with what guile
That fair king's daughter such a beast could tame,
And of his sheathed sword had but little shame.
    But being within the doors, both mantle grey
And heavy gown Medea cast away,
And in thin clinging silk alone was clad,
And round her neck a golden chain she had,
Whereto was hung a harp of silver white.
Then the great dragon, at that glittering sight,
Raised himself up upon his loathly feet,
As if to meet her, while her fingers sweet
Already moved amongst the golden strings,

Preluding nameless and delicious things …
    As thus she sung the beast seemed not to hear
Her words at first, but ever drew anear,
Circling about them, and Medea's face
Grew pale unto the lips, though still the place
Rung with the piercing sweetness of her song;
But slower soon he dragged his length along,
And on his limbs he tottered, till at last
All feebly by the wondering prince he passed,
And whining to Medea's feet he crept,
With eyes half closed, as though well-nigh he slept,
And there before her laid his head adown;
Who, shuddering, on his wrinkled neck and brown
Set her white foot, and whispered: "Haste, O love!
Behold the keys …"

WILLIAM MORRIS, *THE LIFE AND DEATH OF JASON*

THE GARDEN OF THE HESPERIDES

But in the midst there was a grassy space,
Raised somewhat over all the flowery place,
On marble terrace-walls wrought like a dream;
And round about it ran a clear blue stream,
Bridged o'er with marble steps, and midmost there
Grew a green tree, whose smooth grey boughs did bear
Such fruit as never man elsewhere had seen,
For 'twixt the sunlight and the shadow green
Shone out fair apples of red gleaming gold.
Moreover round the tree, in many a fold,
Lay coiled a dragon, glittering little less
Than that which his eternal watchfulness
Was set to guard; nor yet was he alone,
For from the daisied grass about him shone
Gold raiment wrapping round two damsels fair,
And one upon the steps combed out her hair,
And with shut eyes sung low as in a dream;
And one stood naked in the cold blue stream,
While on the bank her golden raiment lay;
But on that noontide of the quivering day,
She only, hearing the seafarers' shout,
Her lovely golden head had turned about,
And seen their white sail flapping o'er the wall,
And as she turned had let her tresses fall,
Which the thin water rippling round her knee
Bore outward from her toward the restless sea.

WILLIAM MORRIS, *THE LIFE AND DEATH OF JASON*

28

European
Dragons

*The power and energy of the dragon caused its adoption in
pagan times as a heraldic device. In the Christian mind its
unruliness represented evil, and its slaying symbolized the
triumph of Christ over the powers of darkness.*

THE FIREDRAKE

Many centuries before the birth of Beowulf, a family of mighty warriors had won by their swords a priceless treasure of weapons and of armour, of richly chased goblets and cups, of magnificent ornaments and precious jewels, and of gold 'beyond the dreams of avarice'. In a great cave among the rocks it was hoarded by the last of their line, and on his death none knew where it was hidden. Upon it one day there stumbled a fiery dragon – a Firedrake – and for three hundred years the monster gloated, unchallenged, over the magnificent possession. But at the end of that time, a bondsman, who fled before his master's vengeance and sought sanctuary in the mountains, came on an opening in the rocks, and, creeping in, found the Firedrake asleep upon a mass of red gold and of sparkling gems that dazzled his eyes even in the darkness. For a moment he stood, trembling, then, sure of his master's forgiveness if he brought him as a gift a golden cup all studded with jewels, he seized one and fled with it ere the monster could awake.

With its wakening, terror fell upon the land. Hither and thither it flew, searching for him who had robbed it, and as it flew, it sent flames on the earth and left behind it a black trail of ruin and death.

JEAN LANG,
A BOOK OF MYTHS

THE TWO DRAGONS

Wishing to construct an impregnable fortress on Salisbury Plain, Vortigern sent for a host of masons, who were dismayed to see the work they had done during the day destroyed every night.

On consulting an astrologer, Vortigern was directed to anoint the stones with the blood of a boy of five who had no human father. The only child corresponding to this description was Merlin, who saved himself from untimely death by telling the King that, if he dug into the earth, and drained the lake which he would find, he would discover broad stones beneath which two dragons slept by day, but fought so fiercely at night that they caused the tremendous earthquakes which shattered his walls. These directions were followed, and the dragons were roused, and fought until the red one was slain and the two-headed white one disappeared. Asked to explain the meaning of these two dragons, Merlin declared that the white dragon with two heads represented the two younger sons of King Constance, who were destined to drive Vortigern away. Having thus spoken, Merlin disappeared, escaping the wrath of Vortigern, who wished to slay him.

Soon after, the young princes surprised and burned Vortigern in his new palace, and recovered possession of their father's throne. Then, one of them dying, the other, assuming both their names, became Uther Pendragon, King of Britain.

HA GUERBER, *THE BOOK OF THE EPIC*

Among the ancient Britons and Welsh the dragon was the national symbol on the war standard; hence the term Pendragon for the dux bellorum, or leader in war (pen = head or chief).

BREWER'S DICTIONARY OF PHRASE AND FABLE

King Arthur and the Questing Beast

S oon they spied a hart before them, which the King claimed as his game, and he spurred his horse and rode after him. But the hart ran fast and the King could not get near it, and the chase lasted so long that the King himself grew heavy and his horse fell dead under him. Then he sat under a tree and rested, till he heard the baying of hounds, and fancied he counted as many as thirty of them. He raised his head to look, and, coming towards him, saw a beast so strange that its like was not to be found throughout his kingdom. It went straight to the well and drank, making as it did so the noise of many hounds baying, and when it had drunk its fill the beast went its way.

ANDREW LANG, *THE BOOK OF ROMANCE*

SIR LAUNCELOT DU LAC

T hen this lady said to Sir Launcelot: Sir, if it please you will ye go with me hereby into a chapel that we may give loving and thanking unto God? Madam, said Sir Launcelot, come on with me, I will go with you. So when they came there and gave thankings unto God all the people, both learned and lewd, gave thankings unto God and him, and said: Sir knight, since ye have delivered this lady, ye shall deliver us from a serpent there is here in a tomb. Then Sir Launcelot took his shield and said: Bring me thither, and what I may do unto the pleasure of God and you I will do. So when Sir Launcelot came thither he saw written upon the tomb letters of gold that said thus: Here shall come a leopard of king's blood, and he shall slay this serpent, and this leopard shall engender a lion in this foreign country, the which lion shall pass all other knights. So then Sir Launcelot lift up the tomb, and there came out an horrible and a fiendly dragon, spitting fire out of his mouth. Then Sir Launcelot drew his sword and fought with the dragon long, and at the last with great pain Sir Launcelot slew that dragon.

ALFRED W. POLLARD, *THE ROMANCE OF KING ARTHUR AND HIS KNIGHTS OF THE ROUND TABLE* (ABRIDGED FROM MALORY)

THE RED CROSS KNIGHT

The dragon lay stretched out on the side of the hill. When it saw the silver armour of the Red Cross Knight shining in the sunshine it roused itself and gave a terible roar which made the ground shake for miles around. Then, slowly uncoiling its great length, it came towards him.

The Red Cross Knight told Una to go away to a little distance where she would be safe. And Una, knowing that he would not want to be hampered now by fears for her safety, obeyed him and rode to the top of a little hill close by, from which she might watch the battle without danger.

The dragon was indeed a dreadful-looking creature. His body was covered with glistening scales like a thick coat of armour. He had two great wings with which he could fly, and his tail was almost three furlongs in length, with two terrible stings at the end. His claws were sharp and strong, and out of his mouth came clouds of smoke and flames of fire ...

Spear in hand, the Red Cross Knight awaited the dragon's coming ... At the first rush the dragon bore him and his steed to the ground, but the knight was quickly on his feet again; and then, with shield and sword and spear, he fought long and bravely against the monster ...

And this time the fight did not last long. For as the dragon came rushing towards the brave knight, with his mouth wide open to swallow him, the knight managed to inflict a fatal wound in the dragon's mouth, his one vulnerable spot.

With a roar that shook the earth for miles around and made even the knight tremble, the dragon fell upon the ground. There he lay like a huge fallen mountain, dead at last. The Red Cross Knight had gained the victory; Una's enemy was defeated; the quest of the Fairy Queen had been performed.

CHRISTINE CHAUNDLER,
MY BOOK OF STORIES FROM THE POETS

DRAGON'S HILL

here is a site in Berkshire where one legend has it that St George killed the dragon. A bare place is shown on the hill, where nothing will grow, and there the blood of the dragon ran out.

In Saxon annals we are told that Cerdic, founder of the West Saxon kingdom, slew there Naud (or Natanleod, the people's refuge), the pendragon, with 5,000 men.

BREWER'S DICTIONARY OF PHRASE AND FABLE

At Burford, in Oxfordshire, Midsummer Eve used to be celebrated with great jollity by the carrying of a giant and a dragon up and down the town.

SIR JAMES FRAZER, *THE GOLDEN BOUGH*

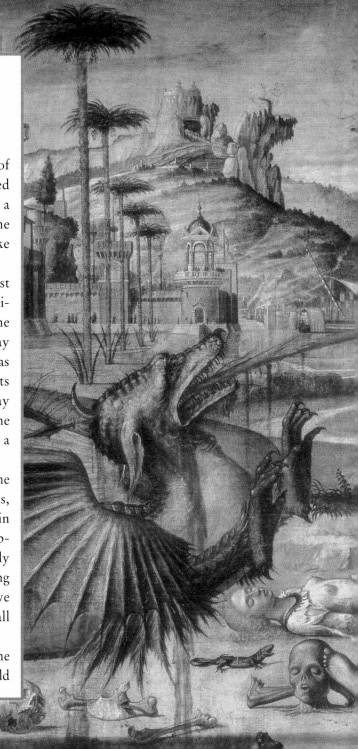

St George and the Dragon

On a time St George came to the city of Silene, which is in the province called Libya. He was a youth of great valour, a soldier, as his father had been before him, in the army of the Roman Emperor Diocletian, and, like his father, a Christian.

And hard by this city of Silene there was a vast stagnant lake, wherein dwelt a dragon, which poisoned all the countryside with its breath. The people assembled more than once in order to slay the beast, yet when it came forth they fled, and as it drew near the city it killed the citizens with its breath, so that they were fain to give it every day two sheep thenceforward, that it might not come nearer, and when the sheep failed they gave it a man and a sheep.

There was a decree made in that city that all the children and the young people should draw lots, one by one, to decide which of them should in turn be delivered to the dragon. And it so happened at last that the lot fell upon the King's only daughter, whose name was Saba, whereof the King was sorry, and he said unto the people, "For love of the gods, take my gold and my silver, and all that I have, and let me keep my daughter!"

They answered, "How, sir! Ye have made the law, and our children are dead, and now you would

break the law you made. Your daughter must be delivered to the dragon."

When the king saw that he might do no more he began to weep, and said to his daughter, "Now I shall never see thee a bride!"

Then the King arrayed his daughter like a bride, and embraced her, and led her to the place where the dragon was.

When she was standing there it so happened that St George rode by, and when he saw her he said, "Lady, what make you here?"

And she answered, "Go ye your way, fair youth, that you perish not also."

Then said he, "Tell me what is amiss, and why you are weeping, and be not afraid."

When she saw that he was resolved to know the truth she told him how she was delivered over to be devoured by the dragon. Then said St George, "Fair damsel, fear not, for in the name of Jesus Christ I will help you."

"For God's love, gentle knight," said the Princess, "get you gone and tarry not with me, for help me you cannot."

Thus as they were speaking together the dragon appeared, and he was terrible to behold, and all the coneys that dwelt among the rocks hid them in their burrows for fear of his breath. When the dragon saw

St George upon his horse he rushed toward him. But St George made the sign of the Cross, and sloped his spear and set in his spurs, and rode boldly against the beast; and his spear drove through the dragon's jaws and into its midriff, and hurt it sore, so that it lay upon the earth.

Then St George said to the Princess, "Bind your girdle about the dragon's neck, and fear not." And she took her girdle, which was of fine broidery and rich goldsmith's work, and girt it about the dragon's neck, and it followed her as if it had been a tame beast and a gentle. And therewith all the coneys crept forth from their burrows, for they were afraid no more.

The Princess led the dragon toward the city, and the people fled, crying, "Alas, we shall all be slain!"

Then said St George to them, "Fear not – believe in God, and in Jesus Christ His son, and be ye baptized, and I will slay the dragon."

Then was the King baptized, and all his people with him, and St George cut off the dragon's head, and the body and the head were borne out of the city on a great cart drawn by four yoke of oxen.

DOROTHY MARGARET STUART, *THE BOOK OF CHIVALRY AND ROMANCE* (ADAPTED FROM THE '*GOLDEN LEGEND*' OF JACOPO DE VORAGINE)

SIGURD AND THE DRAGON

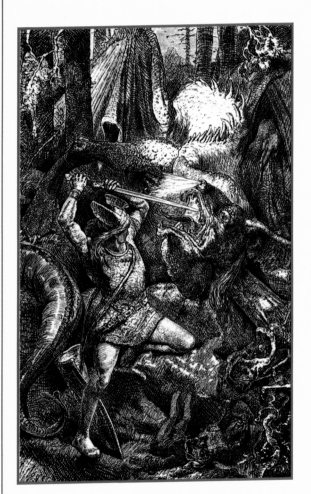

Now crept the worm down to his place of watering, and the earth shook all about him, and he snorted forth venom on all the way before him as he went; but Sigurd neither trembled nor was adrad at the roaring of him. So whenas the worm crept over the pit, Sigurd thrust his sword under his left shoulder, so that it sank in up to the hilt; then up leapt Sigurd from the pit and drew the sword back unto him, and therewith was his arm all bloody, up to the very shoulder.

Now when that mighty worm was ware that he had his death-wound, then he lashed out head and tail, so that all things soever that were before him were broken to pieces.

So whenas Fafnir had his death-wound, he asked, 'Who art thou? and who is thy father? and what thy kin, that thou wert so hardy as to bear weapons against me?' ...

He answered, 'Sigurd am I called, and my father was Sigmund.'

WILLIAM MORRIS,
THE STORY OF THE VOLSUNGS AND NIBLUNGS

eople call them Pterodactyles: but that is only because they are ashamed to call them flying dragons, after denying so long that flying dragons could exist.

CHARLES KINGSLEY, *THE WATER-BABIES*

A Very Different Dragon

he Boy bit off a stalk of grass and chewed it. "Going to make a long stay here?" he asked, politely.

"Can't hardly say at present," replied the dragon. "It seems a nice place enough – but I've only been here a short time, and one must look about and reflect and consider before settling down. It's rather a serious thing, settling down. Besides – now I'm going to tell you something! You'd never guess it if you tried ever so! – fact is, I'm such a confoundedly lazy beggar!"

"You surprise me," said the Boy, civilly.

"It's the sad truth," the dragon went on, settling down between his paws and evidently delighted to have found a listener at last: "and I fancy that's really how I came to be here. You see all the other fellows were so active and earnest and all that sort of thing – always rampaging, and skirmishing, and scouring the desert sands, and pacing the margin of the sea, and chasing knights all over the place, and devouring damsels, and going on generally – whereas I liked to get my meals regular and then to prop my back against a bit of rock and snooze a bit, and wake up and think of things going on just the same, you know!"

KENNETH GRAHAME, *THE RELUCTANT DRAGON*

DRAGONS OF ASIA AND AMERICA

Unlike its psychopathic Western cousin, the Oriental dragon was seen as a divine figure, in whom all the elements were united. Living in lakes and in the sky, symbolizing fertility and creativity, it was regarded with caution and respect.

THE CHINESE DRAGON

"The earth joins up with the dragon"
(CHINESE SAYING, MEANING THAT IT IS RAINING)

nd so the sense of the impermanence of things, and the transitoriness of life, which in Buddhism was allied to human sorrow, became a positive and glowing inspiration.

The soul identified itself with the wind which bloweth where it listeth, with the cloud and the mist that melt away in rain, and are drawn up again into the air; and this sovereign energy of the soul, fluid, penetrating, ever-changing, took form in the symbolic Dragon.

We do not know the origin of this symbol; it is lost in obscure ages. Perhaps not at first, but certainly in early times it was associated with the element of water, with storms discharging rain, with the clouds and the thunder. "Water," says Lao-tzu, "is the weakest and softest of things, yet overcomes the strongest and hardest." It penetrates everywhere subtly, without noise, without effort. So it became typical of the spirit which is able to pass out into all other existences of the world and resume its own form in man; and, associated with the power of fluidity, the Dragon became the symbol of the infinite.

LAURENCE BINYON, *THE FLIGHT OF THE DRAGON*

It is either characteristic of the dragon that it lives in the clouds, gives birth to its young there and never comes down to earth; or it rises up and sinks down, and then it brings its young into the world down here, and when these grow up, they rise up to the clouds. To say that the dragon ascends into the air, implies that it is a spirit; if it were not a spirit, it could not reach the clouds, since it is characteristic of spirits that they ascend so high. But man is nobler than the dragon; how then does it come about that the nobler creature cannot ascend so high, while the lesser and baser can? … Moreover, the dragon possesses an outward appearance and hence moves in a visible manner; if it moves thus, it can also eat; but a being which has an outward appearance, moves visibly and eats, cannot be termed a spirit. Further, is it not commonly said that the dragon is king of the three hundred species of animal? As king of the animal world it must also have a body, since what is a king without a body?

ANON (HAN DYNASTY)

THE DRAGON OF PEARL HARBOUR

In Polynesia the dragon is called mo-o and mo-ko. Their use of this word in traditions showed that they often had in mind animals like crocodiles and alligators, and sometimes they referred the name to any monster of great mythical powers belonging to the man-destroying class. Mighty eels, immense sea-turtles, large fish of the ocean, fierce sharks, were all called mo-o. The most ancient dragons of the Hawaiians are spoken of as living in pools or lakes. … one dragon lived in the Ewa lagoon, now known as 'Pearl Harbour'. This was Kane-kua-ana,

who was said to have brought the pipi (oysters) to Ewa. She was worshipped by those who gather the shell-fish. When the oysters began to disappear about 1850, the natives said the dragon had become angry and was sending the oysters to Kahiki, or some far-away foreign land.

WD WESTERVELT, *LEGENDS OF GODS AND GHOSTS*

A Japanese Dragon-Slayer

After Susa-no-wo had been banished from heaven, he descended on Tori-kami, beside the river Hi, in the province of Idzumo. A chopstick came floating down the river, so that he knew that people were dwelling near, and he set out to search for them. He soon met an old man and an old woman who were weeping bitterly; between them walked a lovely maiden …

"Why do you weep?" asked Susa-no-wo.

Said the old man: "I have had eight daughters, but each year the eight-forked serpent (dragon) of Koshi has come and devoured one after the other. I weep now because the time is at hand to give Kush-inada-hime to the serpent."

"What is the serpent like?"

"Its eyes are red as the winter cherry; it has a body with eight heads and eight tails, and on its body grow moss and trees. It is so long that it stretches over eight valleys and eight hills. Its belly is constantly bloody and inflamed."

"If this maiden is your daughter," said Susa-no-wo, "will you give her to me?"

"You honour me," the old man made answer, "but I do not know your name."

"I am the dear brother of the sun-goddess, and have just descended from heaven."

"Most obediently do I offer my daughter to you," the old man said with reverence.

Susa-no-wo then transformed the girl into a comb, which he placed in his hair. Having done this, he bade the old couple to brew rice-beer (sake). They obeyed him, and he asked them to construct a fence with eight gates and eight benches, and to place on each bench a vat filled with the beer.

In time the eight-forked serpent came nigh. It dipped each of its heads into each of the vats, drank the sake, became drunk, and then lay down and slept. Susa-no-wo drew his two-handed sword, and cut the serpent in pieces. The Hi River turned red with blood.

DONALD A MACKENZIE,
MYTHS OF CHINA AND JAPAN

THE FEATHERED SERPENT

In the ancient civilization of America one of the most prominent deities was called the "Feathered Serpent", in the Maya language, Kukulkan, Quiche Gukumatz, Aztec Quetzalcoatl, the Pueblo "Mother of Waters". Throughout a very extensive part of America the snake, like the Indian Naga, is the emblem of rain, clouds, thunder and lightning. But it is essentially and pre-eminently the symbol of rain; and the god who controls the rain, Chac of the Mayas, Tlaloc of the Aztecs, carried the axe and the thunderbolt like his homologues and prototypes in the Old World. In America also we find reproduced in full, not only the legends of the antagonism between the thunder-bird and the serpent , but also the identification of these two rivals in one composite monster, which is seen in the winged disks, both

in the Old World and the New. Hardly any incident in the history of the Egyptian falcon or the thunder-birds of Babylonia, Greece or India, fails to reappear in America and find pictorial expression in the Maya and Aztec codices.

G ELLIOT SMITH,
THE EVOLUTION OF THE DRAGON

ACKNOWLEDGEMENTS

ILLUSTRATIONS: p20: Siegfried kills Fafner by Arthur Rackham from *Siegfried and the Twilight of the Gods*, p37: Arthur and the Questing Beast by Louis Rhead from *King Arthur and his Knights* by Sir James Knowl, p49: Gorgonzola flies off on her Dragon by HJ Ford, from *The Green Fairy Book* edited by Andrew Lang, p61: by Mo-No-Yuki, from *Ancient Tales and Folklore of Japan* by R Gordon Smith. Illustrations on pp25, 32, 34, 42, 50 and 58 by Andrew Midgley

THE FOLLOWING PICTURES ARE REPRODUCED WITH KIND PERMISSION OF THE BRIDGEMAN ART LIBRARY, LONDON: endpaper & p44/45: St George Killing the Dragon by Vittore Carpaccio. p3: People worship the Dragon, *French Apocalypse* Ms75 f.27v (detail). p7 and back jacket St Michael Killing the Dragon by Meacci, Leicester Gallery, London. p9: Behemoth and Leviathan from *The Book of Job* by William Blake, Fitzwilliam Museum, University of Cambridge. p10: St Michael and the Angels fighting the dragon, Flemish vellum manuscript c.1448. p11 detail (bottom) Dragon Casts out Water, *French Apocalypse*, Lambeth Palace Library, London. p12: St Michael, from the *Tres Riches heures of the Duc de Berry* by Pol Limbourg, Musee Conde, Chantilly. p13: St Nicholas of Bari and St Michael by Fra (Guido di Pietro) Angelico, Sotheby's, London. p14: The Passing of the Soul by Evelyn de Morgan, The de Morgan Foundation, London. p15: detail (left and right) from a tile by William de Morgan, Fitzwilliam Museum, University of Cambridge. p16& 28 The Captives by Evelyn de Morgan, The de Morgan Foundation, London. p17: Perseus rescuing Andromeda by Joachim Wtewael or Utewael, Giraudon, Paris. p18: Details of the Temptation of St Anthony by Mattias Grunewald. p21: Hercules Fighting with the Lernaean Hydra by Francisco de Zurbaran. p22: Perseus and Andromeda by Sir Edward John Poynter, The Fine Art Society, London. p23 and front jacket: Perseus and Andromeda by Frederic. p24: (detail) Apollo about to Attack the Python, engraving by Carracius. p31: St George slaying the dragon, Johann or Hans von Aachen, Phillips, the International Fine Art Auctioneers. p40: St George and the Dragon, Flemish, probably Bruges, c.1500,

Fitzwilliam Museum, University of Cambridge. p41 St George and the Dragon by Peter Paul Reubens, Prado, Madrid. p43: (detail bottom left) Ariadne Ms Fr 874 f.179v, Bibliotheque Nationale, Paris. p47: Fair St George by Sir John Gilbert. p60: A Dragon and Two Tigers by Sadahide, courtesy of the Board of Trustees of The V&A.

THE CAMERON COLLECTION: p36: Arthur dreams of the Dragon by Herbert Cole from Rhys Fairy Tales.

CHRISTIES: p38 St George and the dragon by Armand Point. p51: The Rescue by Arthur Hughes.

E.T. ARCHIVE: p33: (detail) 15th century knight prepares to confront dragon in castle.

FINE ART PHOTOGRAPHIC: p2: The Queen of the Seas by Charles Lepec

HORIZON: c Steve Daw p59: Chinese Embroidery dragon.

THE HUTCHISON LIBRARY: p52 & 53: photographs by Felix Greene. p54: photograph by Christine Pemberton. p55: photograph by Rene-Nicolas Giudicelli.

IMAGES, THE CHARLES WALKER COLLECTION: p57: 18th Century Chinese Symbols-Pearl.

LAMBETH PALACE LIBRARY: p35 MS6, fol 43v with thanks to The Archbishop of Canterbury and the Trustees of Lambeth Palace Library.

SOTHEBY'S TRANSPARENCY LIBRARY, LONDON: p11: Saint George Slaying the Dragon, icon c.1600. p26: *An Autumn Fairy Tale* by Ernst Stohr.

THE VISUAL ARTS LIBRARY, LONDON: p30: Man and dragon, tapestry, Basle Historisches Museum. p43 (top right) Roman de Melusine by Coulderette(?) and Jean d'Arras, Bibli50eque National, Paris. p56:The Skirt of a Mandarin, 19th century Chinese. p63: In the Gem Garden by L. Carre, private collection.